W9-BRS-182

YOUR LAND
AND
MY LAND
ASIA

We Visit

NORTH KOREA

Claire

O'Neal

Mitchell Lane
PUBLISHERS
P.O. Box 196
Hockessin, Delaware 19707

YOUR LAND AND MY LAND
ASIA

Cambodia

China

India

Indonesia

Japan

Malaysia

North Korea

The Philippines

Singapore

South Korea

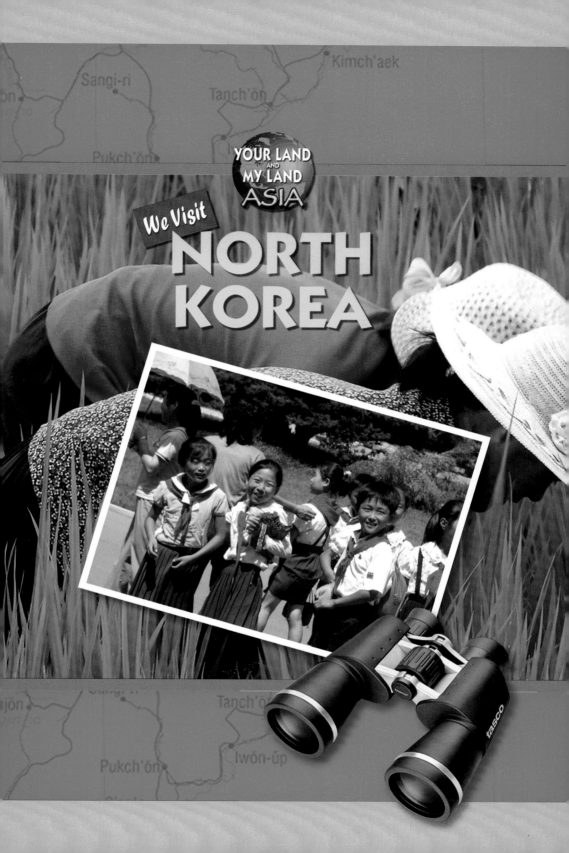

YOUR LAND
AND
MY LAND
ASIA

We Visit

NORTH
KOREA

Printing   1   2   3   4   5   6   7   8   9

Asia

Library of Congress Cataloging-in-Publication Data
O'Neal, Claire.
We visit North Korea / by Claire O'Neal.
      pages cm. — (Your land and my land)
Includes bibliographical references and index.
Audience: Ages 9-13.
ISBN 978-1-61228-480-4 (library bound)
1. Korea (North)—History—Juvenile literature. 2. Korea (North)—Politics and government—Juvenile literature. 3. Korea (North)—Social life and customs—Juvenile literature. I. Title.
DS935.25.O54 2014
951.93—dc23
                                                        2013041469
eBook ISBN: 9781612285351

PUBLISHER'S NOTE: This story is based on the author's extensive research, which she believes to be accurate. Documentation of this research is on page 61. The author also gratefully acknowledges helpful discussions with Youngsang Kwon and Jinhee Oh.

      The internet sites referenced herein were active as of the publication date. Due to the fleeting nature of some websites, we cannot guarantee they will all be active when you are reading this book.

Contents

Introduction

Modern, rich countries pack East Asia, such as China, Japan, Taiwan, and South Korea. But large differences between rich and poor inspired Asians to create some of the world's first communist governments. In communism, ideas such as "rich" and "poor" should be erased, because workers get what they need from the government—homes, food, health care, education. Russia was first, forming the Union of Soviet Socialist Republics (USSR) in 1917. Then China became communist in 1949. Vietnam, Laos, and Cambodia also established communist governments. In each case, however, communism was a hard-fought and bloody battle where many freedoms were lost.

The Korean Peninsula was split in two at the end of World War II. Separate governments in North Korea and South Korea were established in 1948. Since then, the Kim family has kept North Korea ready to fight. Today Kim Jung-un threatens South Korea, Japan, and the United States with nuclear war. But North Korea's borders remain sealed. Few people can come in and even fewer get out. Yet reports trickle in. They all tell of a proud but beaten-down population, living at the mercy of a dangerous dictator.

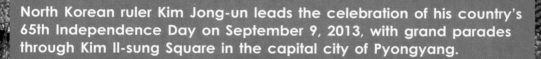

North Korean ruler Kim Jong-un leads the celebration of his country's 65th Independence Day on September 9, 2013, with grand parades through Kim Il-sung Square in the capital city of Pyongyang.

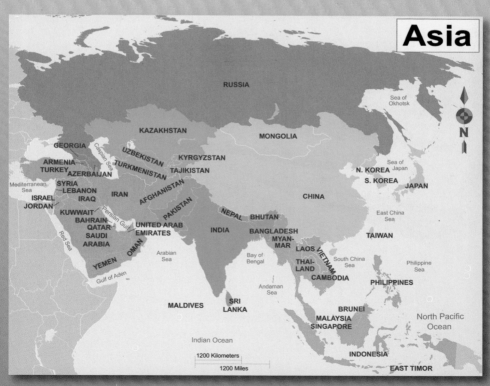

Asia

RUSSIA

KAZAKHSTAN

MONGOLIA

Sea of Okhotsk

GEORGIA

Caspian Sea

UZBEKISTAN

KYRGYZSTAN

ARMENIA

TURKEY

TURKMENISTAN

TAJIKISTAN

AZERBAIJAN

Sea of Japan

N. KOREA

S. KOREA

JAPAN

Mediterranean Sea

SYRIA

LEBANON

IRAN

AFGHANISTAN

CHINA

ISRAEL

IRAQ

JORDAN

PAKISTAN

NEPAL

BHUTAN

East China Sea

KUWWAIT

Persian Gulf

BAHRAIN

UNITED ARAB

EMIRATES

INDIA

BANGLADESH

QATAR

MYAN-

MAR

TAIWAN

SAUDI

ARABIA

OMAN

LAOS

VIETNAM

Red Sea

YEMEN

Arabian Sea

Bay of Bengal

THAI-

LAND

South China Sea

Philippine Sea

Gulf of Aden

CAMBODIA

PHILIPPINES

Andaman Sea

MALDIVES

SRI LANKA

BRUNEI

MALAYSIA

SINGAPORE

North Pacific Ocean

Indian Ocean

1200 Kilometers

1200 Miles

INDONESIA

EAST TIMOR

N

A government propaganda poster displayed in the city of Wonsan shows North Korean soldiers and civilians ready for war and for work.

A Country Split in Two

The dull gray walls of buildings in Pyongyang, North Korea, make the colorful posters that cover them stand out like fireworks for the eyes. One poster shows proud, uniformed school children. They clutch books filled with the writings of the country's founder and Eternal President, Kim Il-sung. Another poster shows happy, rosy-cheeked children next to armored tanks and military rockets. They raise their hands to the sky under the words "Our General, Kim Jong-il [Kim Il-sung's son and successor] is the best!" Portraits of the Kims depict their smiling faces shining with confidence and love, as though they are fathers to everyone.

Most posters show soldiers in green helmets and uniforms, brandishing guns and knives and thirsting for battle. They say "In our opinion, our fighting spirit, our way of living, let's do according to the demands of the military first!" Others show grisly images of American soldiers being stabbed by bayonets or crushed under tanks. One detailed country scene shows a smiling American soldier holding a wailing Korean baby over a well. These posters demand, "Do not forget the American imperialist wolves!"[1]

The North Korean capital city itself is usually a model of quiet efficiency. Citizens walk in neat suits or uniforms to their jobs. They wait patiently for subway trains in museum-clean stations. School children walk, holding hands, in perfect lines. Traffic girls dressed in crisp white or blue uniforms stand where roads intersect, displaying hand signals with robot-like precision. In a country in which only about one out of every 800 people owns a car, however, these traffic girls often perform their jobs in empty streets.[2]

The streets weren't empty on Victory Day 2013. Ten thousand soldiers marched alongside anti-aircraft missiles. Fighter jets and helicopters zoomed loudly over Kim Il-sung Square. Citizens in crisp new uniforms of white, red, and blue carried tall national flags, and worked together to bear life-sized statues of their former leaders.

The celebration marked the 60th anniversary of the end of the Korean War. Sixty-year celebrations receive special honor in Korea, because sixty years marks one complete cycle of the Chinese zodiac calendar. People celebrate a 60th birthday, or *hwangab*, with an enormous party. Kim Jong-un, Kim Il-sung's grandson and the country's current leader, celebrated North Korea's 60th Victory Day in show-stopping style.

Sixty miles (100 kilometers) to the south, poor farmers in North Hwanghae Province knew nothing of Pyongyang's grand parades. Many had been homeless for a year, after twin typhoons struck North Korea in August 2012, killing dozens of people and destroying 6,700 homes.[3] Now they worked feverishly to save their crops from another year of flooding. The rising waters would destroy at least 30,000 acres (12,140 hectares) of crops and kill the season's potato harvest.

The marching and weapons were not just for show. One hundred miles (178 kilometers) south of Pyongyang, hundreds of thousands of highly trained troops stood battle-ready along the Demilitarized Zone,

FYI FACT:

North Korea's national animal is the chollima, a speedy winged horse from Asian myth. On November 29, 2012, archaeologists of the DPRK Academy of Social Sciences announced the "discovery" of the lair of a similar animal—a unicorn—that they claimed was once kept by King Dongmyeong of the ancient Koguryo Kingdom.[4]

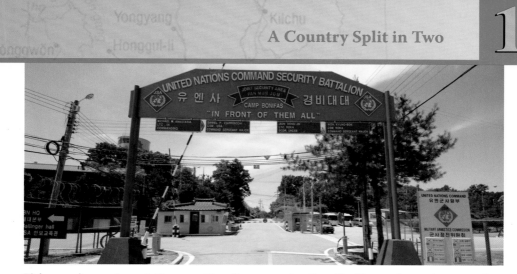

This main gate at Camp Bonifas marks South Korea's entrance to the Korean Demilitarized Zone. The United Nations renamed the camp in 1986 to honor U.S. Army Captain Arthur Bonifas, who was killed by North Korean soldiers.

or DMZ, the world's most heavily guarded international border. Though North Korea and South Korea signed an armistice in 1953 to stop fighting, they never formally agreed to end the Korean War. Today, armies of North Korea and South Korea—and nearly 30,000 American soldiers—stand guard at the border, ready for the Korean War to pick up where it left off.

Life wasn't always like this. Before 1945, there was no North Korea or South Korea. For nearly 1,000 years, the single united kingdom of Choson stood in their place. Koreans on both sides of the border share a history, culture, and language. They also share a dream that one day the people of Choson can once more live together as one.

This dream is far from being realized. South Korea is a world leader in technology and innovation, boasting the highest number of cell phones per person in the world. Meanwhile, North Koreans need candles to light their homes at night, and struggle to fill their hungry stomachs with the meager rations their government provides. Despite his grand parades, the world sees dictator Kim Jong-un as a madman. He threatens the world with nuclear weapons, but does nothing to stop his country from sinking deeper into poverty and starvation.

What happened to split Korea in two? Is there hope for the people of North Korea? Let's take a look behind the iron curtain of North Korea, the most closed-off country in the world, and find out.

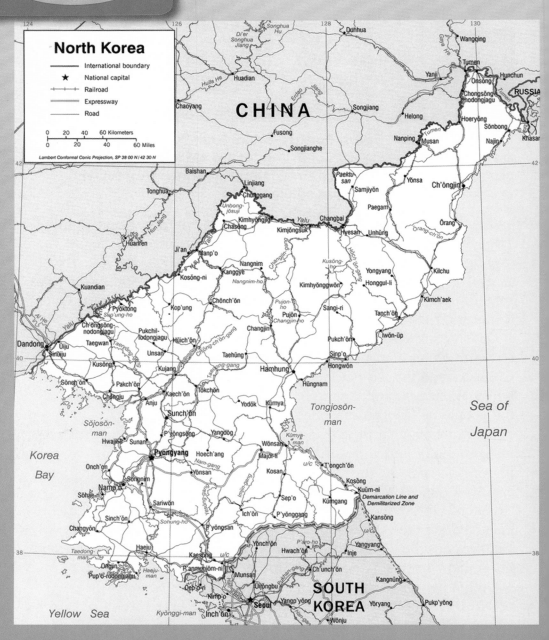

North Korea facts at a glance

Official Country Name: Democratic People's Republic of Korea (DPRK), often called North Korea; formed on September 9, 1948

Capital: Pyongyang

Supreme Leader: Kim Jong-un

Independence: August 15, 1945 (from Japan)

Divisions: 9 provinces (*do*) and 2 special cities (*si*; Pyongyang and Rason)

Land Area: 46,528 square miles (120,540 square kilometers)

Highest Point: Mount Paektu (*Paektu-san*), 9,003 feet (2,744 meters)

Lowest Point: Sea level (0 feet/0 meters)

Population: 24,720,407 (July 2013 estimate)

Ethnic Groups: Korean

Language: Korean (official)

Religion: Discouraged by the government, but people practice Buddhism, Confucianism, some Christianity, and Chondogyo ("Religion of the Heavenly Way")

Government: Communist dictatorship

Currency: North Korean won

Agricultural products: Rice, corn, potatoes, soybeans; livestock such as cattle, pigs, chickens

Major exports: Minerals and metals, manufactured goods, weapons, textiles, fish

Major imports: Oil, coal, machines and equipment, grain

National anthem: *"Aegukka"* ("The Patriotic Song")

Flag: The stripes of the flag symbolize peace (blue), socialism (red), and purity of ideas (white). The five-pointed star represents the Korean Workers' Party, surrounded by a traditional Korean symbol for the universe (white circle).

National Flower: Magnolia

National animal: Chollima, a mythical winged horse

Source: CIA: *The World Factbook*, October 28, 2013
https://www.cia.gov/library/publications/the-world-factbook/geos/kn.html

Lake Chon, or "Heavenly Lake," sits atop Mount Paektu. Lake Chon is so high—7,182 feet (2,190 meters)—and so cold (with an average yearly temperature of 17°F, or -8.3°C) that a blanket of ice often covers it between October and June.

Land of the Morning Calm

The Korean peninsula juts out just 684 miles (1,100 kilometers)—about three-fourths of the length of California—like a thumb under the fat fist of China, with the Sea of Japan to its east and the Yellow Sea to its west. North Korea itself takes up slightly more than half of the peninsula. Its 46,528 square miles (120,540 square kilometers) is about the size of Pennsylvania. Beautiful, high, and cold, North Korea stands set apart from the world, and not just because of its politics.

North Korea is a rugged and mountainous country, with 80% of its land covered by peaks and uplands.[1] The morning mist over mountain valleys has inspired Koreans since ancient times to call their country Choson, or "Land of the Morning Calm." Black and brown bears and even tigers roam the hills in search of prey like sable and deer. The snowy and forbidding Hamgyong Range rises high in the northeast, running east to west not far from the Chinese border. The Rangnim Mountains in central North Korea stretch from north to south. The scenic Taebaek Mountain Range runs like a spine on the eastern side of the peninsula, crossing the border into South Korea. These peaks also provide rich mineral resources, but make transportation across the country difficult.

North Korea's highest point, the picture-perfect, waterfall-covered Mount Paektu, is a national symbol, the mythical birthplace of Korean civilization. It rises 9,003 feet (2,744 meters) along the border with China. Though its Korean name means "white-headed mountain," Mount Paektu is actually an active volcano. Lake Chon at the top

The Sino-Korean Friendship Bridge (right) across the Yalu River allows authorized cars and trains to enter North Korea. Broken Bridge, on the left, was bombed during the Korean War and never repaired.

shimmers with a ring of snow as the highest crater lake in the world.[2] Mount Paektu's last eruption in 1903 was relatively small, but a massive blast around 1000 CE spewed ash as far away as northern Japan.

Melting snow from Mount Paektu feeds both the Tumen River and the Yalu River, which together carve out North Korea's natural border with China. The Tumen River flows east from Mount Paektu to empty into the Sea of Japan, tracing North Korea's tiny, 11-mile (17.5-kilometer) border with Russia along its way. The Yalu River, North Korea's longest, flows west from Mount Paektu to the Yellow Sea. In the 20th century, the Japanese dammed the Yalu in several places, providing North Korea with hydroelectric power. The historic Sino-Korean Friendship Bridge ("Sino" meaning "Chinese"), built by the Japanese between 1937 and 1942, crosses the Yalu to link Dandong, China with Sinuiju, North Korea. A new one is being built to replace it. But along most of their reaches, these northern rivers grow narrow and shallow. They often freeze in the winter under a blanket of snow.

The beauty of the mountains is too harsh for many people. Over half of North Koreans live on the wide, flat plain that stretches along the west coast. This landscape includes Pyongyang (pop. 2,581,076), the capital and most populous city. Because Pyongyang sits more than 30 miles (50 kilometers) inland along the deep Taedong River, its many industries depend on North Korea's largest port city, Nampo (pop. 310,864), where the Taedong meets the Yellow Sea.

A narrower plain along the east coast is home to cities like Hamhung (pop. 614,198), a center of industry on the Songchon River, and the industrial port and former steel-producing center of Chonjin (pop. 614,892). Wonsan (pop. 328,467) boasts beautiful Songdowon Beach, which Kim Jong-un wants to develop into North Korea's first world-class resort.[3] Birdwatchers would enjoy the coasts as well, as a haven for migrating birds such as the Baikal teal, white-naped crane, and white-bellied woodpecker from Japan and mainland Asia.

North Korea has a temperate climate with four seasons. The warm, humid summer months in July and August bring temperatures that hold steady throughout the peninsula, ranging from 70°–80°F (21°–27°C). Winters here feel long and bitterly cold, as a chilly, dry monsoon from mainland Asia drops temperatures as low as -5°F (-21°C) at the peak of Mount Paektu in January and February. East coast winters, protected from the monsoon by Korea's high mountains, feel milder, with lows near 35°F (2°C).

Rain can be unpredictable and even dangerous. Annual precipitation varies greatly, between 30 to 60 inches (75–150 centimeters), depending on the region and the year. Droughts in the late spring are often followed by severe flooding during the summer monsoon season. Most rainfall comes during July or August, when the Korean Peninsula is hit by one or two typhoons. Twin typhoons slammed the Korean Peninsula in the same week in August 2012 with damaging winds and record rainfall. The flooding, landslides, and swollen rivers destroyed homes and crops the country could not afford to lose.

FYI FACT:

As we say "Mount Paektu," Koreans say *Paektu-san*, where *-san* means "mountain." Look for these suffixes in place names on the North Korean map:

City: *-si*   Hill: *-bong*
Village: *-ri*   River: *-gang*
County: *-ju*   Island: *-do*
Neighborhood: *-dong*

A woman enjoys the *darye*, or Korean tea ceremony, in Paris, France. She follows simple steps to heat the water and pour it first into the tea pot, and then her companions' cups. With fewer rules than other Asian tea ceremonies, a *darye* encourages relaxation, conversation, and friendship.

The Rise of Choson

All Korean children know the legend of how their people came to be. In the beginning, the god Hwanin ruled the universe with his sons. One of those sons, Hwanung, peered down at the earth, curious about its people. What he saw saddened him. They seemed lost, without food, law, or hope.

"Father," Hwanung asked, "Could I descend to earth and help them?" Hwanin gave his permission, and searched for a home for his son. When Hwanin found Mount Paektu, he sent his son and 3,000 followers down to rule the Earth. Hwanung taught the people how to grow food, raise animals, and fish; to read and write; to heal their sick; and even to enjoy life with art, dance, and music. His just and fair laws helped everyone live and work together in harmony.

Soon even the wild creatures could not help but wonder at the perfect society Hwanung had made. A bear and a tiger prayed that Hwanung would make them human, too. "First you must prove your worthiness," Hwanung told them. "You must remain in a cave for one hundred days, eating nothing but bitter sacred herbs. If you can suffer through this, you will be worthy to live among my people."

Hungry and impatient, the tiger did not last long. The humble she-bear succeeded. After one hundred days had passed, the bear woke up, but had been transformed into a beautiful woman. Hwanung chose her for his queen. Their son, Dangun Wanggeom, began his reign in 2333 BCE. He ruled over the Choson nation for 1,500 years from Pyongyang. When Dangun's time on earth had ended, he returned to

1992년 2월 16일 새김

Hangul writing on Hyangdo Peak proclaims "Mount Paektu—
Holy Mountain of the Revolution." February 16, 1992 marked
dictator Kim Jong-il's 51st birthday.

Mount Paektu and became an immortal mountain-spirit, reunited in the afterlife with his heavenly family.

Archaeological evidence shows that people arrived on the peninsula much earlier than Dangun. The oldest human fossils date as far back as 350,000 years.[1] By 2000 BCE, early Koreans were making pottery and useful metal objects.

Little is known of specific events in Korean history until 108 BCE, when commanders from the Han Dynasty of China conquered the land. The Chinese were no strangers to Choson. They had already spread their culture and learning throughout the kingdom. Chinese writing influenced the development of Korea's own language. But native Korean tribes opposed their powerful rulers. Constant attacks by the Koreans chipped away at foreign rule until the Chinese withdrew in 57 BCE.

The peninsula entered into the Three Kingdoms period. Silla (founded in 57 BCE) and Paekche (founded in 18 BCE) shared control in the south. The larger and more advanced Koguryo (founded in 37 BCE) controlled the north, which encompassed all of modern-day North Korea as well as some of Manchuria. Though their rulers differed, people throughout the Three Kingdoms shared the same ethnicity, language, and culture. When Buddhism passed from China into Korea in the 3rd century CE, it became the official religion of all three nations. With help from Chinese allies during the Tang Dynasty, Silla—the wealthiest of the three—conquered the other two kingdoms in 668.[2]

The powerful warrior Taejo united the entire peninsula in 936 and founded the Koryo Dynasty. It lasted four centuries, and today lends its name to the English word Korea. Koryo's capital (today's city of Kaesong) was famous throughout the region as a trading center. Buddhism flourished and inspired Koryo inventors to create the world's first printing press in 1234, dedicated to printing the complete works of Buddha. Koryo ceramics makers were master craftsmen. Their pieces feature intricate designs and a special celadon glaze, still prized by art museums today. Koryo survived nearly constant foreign invasions. However, they could not survive an attack from within. In 1392, general Yi Song-gye seized the throne and began a dynasty of his own. He named it Choson after the ancient kingdom of legend.

Despite its violent beginning, Choson brought a golden age of peace, prosperity, and independence to the peninsula. Choson embraced Confucianism, which prizes learning, social order, and respecting your rulers. Scholars set up a formal Korean alphabet, later known as Hangul, and became masters of astronomy. Choson nobility created the *darye*, or Korean tea ceremony, still practiced to this day. Choson rulers established *Kyongguk taejon*, a code of law that controlled every aspect of life and gave the king absolute power.

 Ancient Koreans honored their dead by building dolmen at burial sites. Over 35,000 of these large, slab-rock tables still stand around the peninsula.

The USS *General Sherman* brought American goods in an ill-fated trading mission to Pyongyang in 1866. In response to the attack on the ship, in 1871 the U.S. sent a small navy force to Korea that captured some forts and killed over 200 Korean troops.

The Foreign Fate of the Hermit Kingdom

Especially important among these new laws was a policy of isolation. Choson sought to protect its way of life by keeping to itself, after invasions by the Japanese in the 1590s, and by the Manchu from China in the first half of the 17th century. In the 18th and 19th centuries, the Industrial Revolution sent countries throughout the world in search of new markets for their products. Choson would have none of it, earning the nickname of "Hermit Kingdom" for refusing to trade.

During the late 18th century, foreign powers noticed Choson's strength and wealth, and especially its desirable resources like coal and iron. First the British came calling, then the Russians and the French. Even the Americans tried to force Korea to open up. In 1866, the USS *General Sherman*, loaded with merchandise, sailed up the Taedong River into Pyongyang. Choson soldiers burned the ship and slaughtered the crew.

Though fierce, Choson could not stand for long. Russia demanded access to Choson's warmer ports for its ships. Japan craved Choson's fertile farmland. The two countries went to war over Choson in February 1904. The conflict ended the following year, and the emboldened Japanese claimed the entire peninsula.

The Japanese treated Koreans as second-class citizens in their own country. New laws required Koreans to speak Japanese, and to give up Buddhism and Confucianism and worship instead at Shinto temples. Korean men were drafted into the Japanese army. Parents were even encouraged to change their children's Korean names to Japanese ones.[1]

Angry students rallied two million Koreans in demonstrations throughout the peninsula on March 1, 1919. Protestors quickly met silent, violent ends at the tip of the Japanese sword. Koreans felt defeated and hopeless, but also angry.

Japan's defeat in World War II brought welcome freedom to Korea on August 15, 1945, a day observed throughout Korea as a national holiday. But other countries worried that a newly independent Korea would be unstable. The United Nations voted to temporarily split the peninsula in two along the 38th parallel. The Soviet Union provided resources and assistance to the northern half, while the United States did the same for the south.

Hatred between these two superpowers fueled them to develop their Korean territories into two completely different governments. On August 15, 1948, the Soviet-backed North declared itself the Democratic People's Republic of Korea, a communist dictatorship under the leadership of Kim Il-sung. Meanwhile, the U.S.-backed South held elections to create an American-friendly democracy. Each side proclaimed itself to be the rightful government of the entire peninsula; neither side recognized the other's right to rule.

In the North, Kim Il-sung plotted to unify the peninsula. His People's Army invaded South Korea on June 25, 1950. Northern forces soon controlled nearly all of Korea. U.S. President Harry Truman feared the spread of communism. He convinced the United Nations to provide military support to South Korea's outnumbered army. It was the first time the U.N. would participate in a war, though most of the troops were Americans.

FYI FACT:

U.S. President Theodore Roosevelt won the 1906 Nobel Peace Prize for his role in negotiating the Treaty of Portsmouth to end the Russo-Japanese War. The treaty gave Japan complete control of Korea.

The U.S. Air Force targeted North Korean railroads during the Korean War, such as these train cars south of Wonsan on the east coast.

The famous World War II General Douglas MacArthur directed his troops to attack behind North Korean lines. His strategy worked brilliantly at the Battle of Inchon in September 1950. Two months later, North Korean forces had retreated almost as far as the Chinese border. But 200,000 Chinese troops rushed over the border to North Korea's aid, erasing MacArthur's gains. By March 1951, the North had regained control of their territory. With no clear end in sight, North and South Korea agreed to a cease-fire on July 27, 1953. Because the agreement was not a peace treaty, the two Koreas are still technically at war.

The Korean War devastated the peninsula. Over 1.2 million soldiers from both sides died.[2] Worse was the violence that the Koreans inflicted on each other. North Korea forced 400,000 South Koreans to join the People's Army.[3] They executed any government workers, doctors, or educated people suspected of loyalty to South Korea, which in turn executed as many as 100,000 Koreans believed to be communists. More than 1.5 million civilians also lost their lives.[4] Koreans on both sides crawled through rubble to rebuild roads, railroads, bridges, dams, buildings, and homes destroyed by three years of air strikes and gunfire.

North Korean farmers work in the Rason Free Trade and Economic Zone in 2012. North Korea grows rice, corn, potatoes, beans, tobacco, and tree fruit like apples, peaches, and pears.

The Democratic People's Republic of Korea and Juche

Kim Il-sung believed that North Korea's only chance for survival was to rally behind a strong leader, a dictator—him. He invented *juche* (joo-SHAY), a catchy slogan for his new government. In Korean, "*juche*" means "subject," like the subject of a painting. But to Kim Il-sung, the word meant "Korea First." Kim refused to depend on trade with outsiders for food, products, or services. According to *juche*, North Korea must produce everything its people needed. *Juche* meant that North Korea became a new Hermit Kingdom. But this time, its borders kept people in, not just out. North Koreans who tried to leave the country could be imprisoned or killed. They could not communicate with anyone outside, including relatives in South Korea.

From the outside, Kim Il-sung's Democratic People's Republic of Korea actually looked like a model country offering rights and freedoms. The DPRK constitution proclaims that North Koreans have freedom of speech, freedom of the press, freedom of religion, and freedom to demonstrate against the government. The government also grants the right to work and to rest, the right for all citizens 17 years or older to vote, equal rights for men and women, special privileges for mothers and children, and free education and medical care.[1]

But these rights are only allowed if they do not conflict with *juche*. Kim conveniently accused his enemies of working against *juche*. He assigned *songbun*, or a status in society, to reward people loyal to his Workers' Party. Those with relatives outside of North Korea—especially in Japan or South Korea—or those who had fought against him in the

A rocket is launched from the Sohae Space Center in North Pyongan Province on December 12, 2012. It carried a communications satellite into orbit.

Korean War, were given lower *songbun*. They, and up to three generations of their relatives, could be marked for life as disloyal. People with low *songbun* would never be admitted into the best schools nor get the best jobs. For the slightest slip-ups, they could be sent to nightmarish prison camps, punished with hard labor, starvation, torture, and often death. In many cases, their families, even children, would be sent to prison camp as well.

Though brutal, *juche* seemed to work. North Korea recovered from the war more quickly than the South. But "Korea First" was a lie. Money from North Korea's allies, the Soviet Union and China, funded every building, farm, or factory; their imported food helped feed North Korea's people. When the Soviet Union collapsed in 1991, these vital shipments stopped cold. At the same time, China shifted away from Kim Il-sung, choosing instead to modernize and open trade with the United States. Terrible weather in the early 1990s brought droughts and floods that ruined what few crops North Korea could harvest, already too little to support the population.

As democratic South Korea flourished, North Korea's economy collapsed like a popped balloon. Busy factories fell silent. North Koreans used grass to make weak soup to fill their aching bellies. When Kim Il-sung died suddenly of a heart attack on July 9, 1994, North Koreans collapsed with sorrow, weeping openly in the streets. They faced an uncertain future without their country's founder and only leader for over 50 years. They whispered in fear as his son, the little-known Kim Jong-il, stepped into his father's big shoes.

Kim Jong-il stuck fast to *juche*. North Koreans remained shut out and shut off, helpless, starving. Two and a half million people—one out of every ten North Koreans—died quietly in the famine of the early 1990s, silenced behind their country's closed doors. Meanwhile, the government-controlled Korean Central Broadcasting Station filled TVs with happy faces shouting "We have nothing to envy!" Kim Jong-il ruled for 17 years until he, too, died of a heart attack in 2011.

Kim Jong-un, Kim Jong-il's third son, rules North Korea today. Kim Jong-un claims he wants to unify Korea, but his actions tell a different story. He detonated North Korea's third nuclear weapon in February 2013. Kim used the bomb in a strategy known as brinksmanship, again and again—a dangerous game of blackmail—to get other countries to give him what he wants, usually much-needed aid for his people. Kim Jong-il used brinksmanship, then again and again threatening South Korea, Japan, and the U.S. with missiles and nuclear weapons.

World powers grow tired of this game, like putting up with a spoiled child. South Korea's new president, Park Geun-hye, vowed to wipe the Kim family "off the face of the earth."[3] Even North Korea's closest ally, China, urged Kim Jong-un to back down from his threats. Kim's game is obvious, and yet more dangerous than ever, because it works. After 60 years of absolute Kim family control, North Koreans remain isolated, and *juche* intact.

Kim Il-sung (left) and Kim Jong-il (right), pictured in front of Lake Chon on Mount Paektu in 1994.

The Chinese philosopher Confucius (551–479) encouraged education in ancient Asia. Confucius also taught that society worked best when people obeyed higher authority—like a wife obeying a husband, a son obeying a father, or a subject obeying a prince.

The Culture and Religion of the Kims

Kim Jong-un spends billions of dollars on nuclear weapons while factories fall apart and his people starve. And yet, 20 years after Kim Il-sung's death, every North Korean wears a pin bearing his portrait. Pictures of him hang in every house. When asked, North Koreans burst with pride for their country and its leaders. Why not vote for different leaders? Why not overthrow the Kims? The answer is as complicated as it is terrifying. North Korean culture is a product of hundreds of years of Korean custom and tradition, all carefully manipulated to center on the Kim family.

During the Japanese occupation, Korean scholars rallied their countrymen with the idea of *minjok*, or a "race-nation." *Minjok* gives both Koreas—North and South—a sense of pride. The Korean Peninsula is one of the largest, most ethnically similar societies in the world. DNA evidence shows that Koreans have been a genetically separate people for a long time, even from other Asian populations. Their shared race, culture, and history fuel everyone's desire for the countries to reunite.

But South Korea, with its eyes open towards global travel and trade, moves slowly away from *minjok*. While diversity there increases daily, North Korea heads in the opposite direction. North Korea's policy of isolation outlaws immigration. Only a few hundred foreigners—small pockets of Chinese and Japanese—live in North Korea today. Because North Koreans do not know any other races, it is easy for the Kims to tell the pure-blooded North Koreans that they are cleanest race in

Taeung Hall is part of the Anguk-sa Buddhist Temple in South Pyongan Province. The temple dates back to 503, during the Koguryo Dynasty.

the world, and that all outsiders are evil.[1] Americans hold a special role as the ultimate villains. The long memories of the Korean War's oldest survivors hold stories of Koreans killed by American troops. North Korean propaganda—government-created ads and TV and radio shows—constantly tells North Koreans that, without their strong leaders, their pure and innocent people certainly will fall prey to the Americans lurking at the border.[2]

Like many other Asian cultures, Koreans are extremely concerned with the reputation—the *kibun*—that their name carries in society. The word *kibun* means face, like "saving face" in English.[3] Koreans can hardly think of a worse fate than being publicly insulted or humiliated. To be the bad-mannered person hurling the insults is just as bad. The most honorable Koreans keep their emotions, including their facial expressions, under control. To insult their leaders in public, even if they are bullies, would dishonor a North Korean's entire family.

In North Korea, *kibun* can mean the difference between life and death. The Workers' Party requires the *imminban*, or neighborhood group, to hold regular meetings in which everyone is encouraged to report even the slightest sign of disloyalty, such as not reporting to work on time or traveling to visit relatives without permission from your *imminban*. North Koreans with bad *kibun* fear that the mobile police, or *kyuch'aldae*, will barge into their houses day or night, ready to haul anyone to prison camp if they find so much as a shoe purchased without permission, or a radio that is tuned to a South Korean station.[4]

On paper, the DPRK allows North Koreans freedom of religion. The Kingdom of Choson first practiced Buddhism, a peace-seeking religion founded in India around 500 BCE, and Confucianism, with its roots in China at about the same time. For thousands of years, Koreans have also believed in natural spirits or gods that helped or hindered them. The government encourages groups like the Korean Federation of Buddhists and the Korean Federation of Christians to hold worship services. Kim Il-sung himself promoted two Christian ministers, including his uncle, to high-level political positions. He oversaw the rebuilding of beautiful and historic Buddhist temples destroyed during the Korean War.

But Kim Il-sung regularly called religion unscientific nonsense. In 1992, North Korea changed its constitution to specifically forbid any religion that brings foreign thoughts and ideas into Korea. Houses of worship remain mostly empty out of fear. But deeply held traditions are hard to shake. Buddhism praises those who suffer, such as through famine and hard work. Confucianism insists on loyalty to one's country and the highest respect for rulers. Perhaps the DPRK actually uses Koreans' spiritual beliefs against them, to help the Kims stay in power.

Buddha statue

FYI FACT:

Most Buddhists celebrate their birthdays on the Buddha's birthday, in late April or May. In a similar tradition, North Koreans do not celebrate their own birthdays, but consider themselves a year older on Kim Il-sung's birthday, April 15. It is the one day each year when the electricity stays on, and North Koreans can expect meat in their food packages. Kim Jong-un held lavish festivals on the 100th "Day of the Sun" in 2012—Kim Il-sung was born in 1912—spending an estimated $2 billion.[5]

The Supung Dam between North Korea and China is the largest hydroelectric power station on the Yalu River. Much of the original dam, built by Japanese forces between 1937 and 1941, was destroyed by American bombers during the Korean War.

Nuclear-Powered Economy

North Korea sees itself as a strong and prosperous nation with the raw materials for greatness. Its people are young and well-educated. The fertile land grows rice, potatoes and sweet potatoes, wheat and buckwheat, cabbage, and fruits like apples and pears. Shellfish from the Yellow Sea, especially valuable blue crab, provide a delicious resource to fishermen. The lovely mountains could easily lure tourist dollars, and also burst with rich minerals like gold, copper, magnesium ore, and coal.[1]

But instead of soaring, North Korea's economy sinks. Factories in Chonjin and Hamhung used to manufacture chemical fertilizer, steel products, and vinalon—North Korea's own invented synthetic fabric.[2] Today those factories mostly stand empty, rusting and gutted of valuable parts. Only 2% of the land is permanently farmed.[3] The average North Korean worker makes just $960 annually, down from $1,160 in 1990.[4]

Just beyond the DMZ, the average South Korean worker made $42,255 in 2009, more than doubling the 1990 average. Today, South Korea is a major player in the global economy and society. Whether manufacturing world-class electronics and cars, or playing baseball and strutting their "Gangnam Style," South Koreans enjoy democracy, free trade, and many personal freedoms.

In contrast, North Korea operates as a totalitarian communist dictatorship. Every aspect of its economy—and of people's everyday lives—is strictly controlled by Kim Jong-un and the Workers' Party.

North Korean fishermen work from boats on the Yalu River on April 11, 2013, to catch the river's abundant carp and eel.

The DPRK runs all businesses and construction sites and decides what products the country will manufacture in its factories. The government also owns all the land and chooses which crops will be grown. At harvest time, all crops go to a central food bank that distributes the food in exchange for a job well done. But North Korea's farms cannot produce enough food to feed its people, leading to food shortages and widespread hunger. Fish caught from the Yellow Sea and the Sea of Japan provide an important source of protein. But with few trucks or drivable roads, it can be difficult to bring any goods—let alone easily spoiled fish—to people living far from the coasts.

A large part of North Korea's downfall is that Kim Jong-un cannot provide his people with reliable electricity. North Korea lacks the money, parts, and training to repair its Soviet-constructed power plants. Transportation of its own coal and oil reserves is difficult when railways lie in disrepair. Major dams along the Yalu River provide much-needed hydroelectric power, but this international-border electricity must be shared with China, and lies far away from North Korea's industrial centers.

North Korea has borrowed electricity to power factories as international partnerships. Since the 1990s, factories making clothes and packing goods to ship across the Sea of Japan have run on Chinese power in the far northeast port town of Sonbong. In 2002, the Kaesong Industrial Region opened new doors between North and South Korea. Factories there manufacture clothes, shoes, and watches for South Korean brands, as well as parts for Hyundai cars.

Early on, Kim Il-sung realized North Korea needed cheap and reliable power—nuclear power—to succeed. Soviet scientists and engineers helped him build the Yongbyon Nuclear Scientific Research Center between 1965 and 1985. In return, Kim Il-sung agreed to the Nuclear Nonproliferation Treaty in 1985, pledging never to turn fuel from the nuclear power plants into nuclear weapons. But he went back on his word. By 1993, international observers suspected that North Korea was removing radioactive plutonium from its nuclear reactor. In October 2002, North Korea admitted to building nuclear bombs with fuel from the power plant.

The news stunned the world. How could Kim Jong-il spend so much money building expensive nuclear weapons while his people starved? The U.S. and other countries threatened economic sanctions—restrictions on aid—unless North Korea stopped. Representatives from the U.S., China, Russia, Japan, South Korea, and North Korea met on August 9, 2003, in the first of many Six-Nation talks to try to keep Kim Jong-il from starting a nuclear war. After two years of negotiations, North Korea promised to stop developing nuclear weapons, in exchange for much-needed aid for its people. A year later, North Korea detonated its first nuclear weapon. Again, the world imposed sanctions, until Six-Nation talks in 2007 agreed to provide $400 million in aid if North Korea stopped its dangerous game. North Korea continues to break its promises. It detonated a second nuclear weapon in 2009, and a third in 2013. Instead of helping its starving, desperate people, the rogue country holds the world hostage to get what it wants.

FYI FACT:

North Korea may be one of the world's largest manufacturers of counterfeit U.S. money. In the 1980s, Kim Jong-il bought expensive printing presses that use the same technology as the U.S. Mint. U.S. Treasury experts estimate that the Kim family uses billions of fake dollars to finance its wealthy lifestyle and give America another headache.[5]

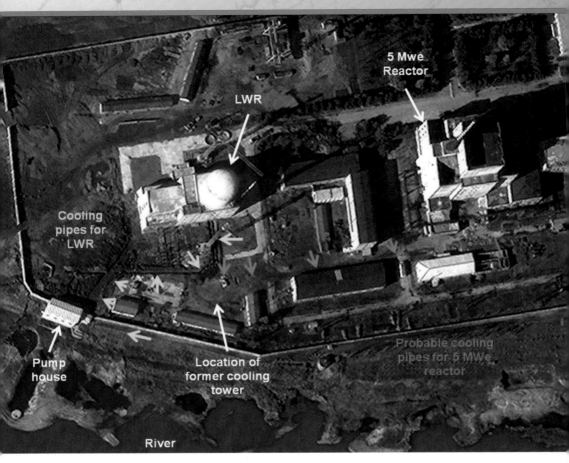

5 Mwe Reactor

LWR

Cooling pipes for LWR

Pump house

Location of former cooling tower

Probable cooling pipes for 5 MWe reactor

River

Satellite reports as recently as this one in November 2012 suggest that suspicious activity continues at North Korea's Yongbyon Nuclear Complex.

No one knows how the Kims pay for these nuclear weapons. In fact, the very nature of money in this Communist state is largely unknown. The North Korean won—the basic unit of currency—is a rare sight in rural areas. Much of North Korea's profits probably come from building and exporting weapons to dangerous or unstable countries. North Korea's first successful mid-range missile test in 1993 frightened South Korea and Japan with fears of war. But its weapons earned free advertising in international news. Countries like Iran, Iraq, Afghanistan, and Yemen lined up to trade, leading President George W. Bush to name North Korea as part of an "axis of evil" in 2002.

Meanwhile, no one can guarantee that international aid money gets to the hungry farmers. The DPRK received nearly $120 million in aid in 2011 from foreign countries, mostly in food.[6] Many suspect that Kim Jong-il used the food to feed his troops instead. He drank French wines and spent hundreds of thousands of dollars to feed his pet dogs. Instead of spending aid money to improve agriculture and soil, Kim Jong-un hopes today to build a ski resort and a horseback-riding club near Pyongyang for his rich friends.

Negotiators hold hands to show their unity at Six-Party talks on February 13, 2007. From left to right: Japan's chief negotiator Kenichiro Sasae, South Korea 's Chun Yung-woo, North Korea's Kim Kye-gwan, China's Wu Dawei, the United States's Christopher Hill, and Russia's Alexander Losyukov.

Boys bicycling in a Pyongyang alley wear the distinctive red scarf of the Young Pioneer Corps, which is open to young people between the ages of 9 and 15.

Training
Young Pioneers

Because the DPRK requires that all children between ages 4 and 15 attend school, its literacy rate is one of the highest in the world. Nearly all adult North Koreans can read the Korean language, known as hangul. Hangul has 24 letters, grouped into block-shaped syllables, which are then written from left to right to form whole words.

North Koreans begin school as young as 4 months. Many go to government daycares where they play, sing, and dance while their parents work. When they are four or five, kindergarteners walk to the school closest to their house, dressed in government-provided uniforms. They prepare for People's School, where 6- to 10-year-olds learn language and literature, math, and Korean history. Many lessons in People's School come from the writings of Kim Il-sung. Even the youngest students must memorize and recite many parts of the Great Leader's works. When they turn nine, the brightest and most loyal children (or those from the best families) join the Young Pioneer Corps and wear the coveted red scarf. These model citizens clean up trash, star in parades, and lead Tree Planting Day each year on March 2.

After People's School comes six years of middle school, where students take subjects like politics, computers, science, and foreign languages, especially English. North Korea encourages students to pursue arts and culture like drama, calligraphy, painting, dance, and music. Good singing is especially prized. From a very early age children are taught traditional folk songs like "Arirang" as well as North Korean propaganda tunes like "The General is our Father." Because North

The Mangyondae Children's Palace in Pyongyang offers exceptional educational opportunities to its students.

Koreans love sports, teachers encourage students to participate in favorites like wrestling, basketball, soccer, gymnastics, and the Korean martial art of taekwondo.

Though all North Koreans have equal rights under the law, only children of Workers' Party officials or successful businesspeople attend the very best middle schools. Specialized middle schools focus on science, foreign language, sports, or military training. One of the most famous is the Children's Palace in Pyongyang, which invites talented (or wealthy) students to pursue lessons with top teachers in arts, sports, foreign languages, and science.

After middle school, young peoples' lives belong to the government, which plots out their next move. Many young men, and some women, go into military service. North Korea's million-man army—fourth-largest in the world—needs a constant supply of recruits. They serve for 10 years, and many consider it an honor to do more. A few promising graduates, usually from specialized middle schools, study at large universities like Kim Il-sung University in Pyongyang. Smaller colleges around the country specialize in teacher training. But most young people simply go to work. Decisions about each citizen's job—whether farmer, factory worker, or pharmacist—are made by the government. No one gets to choose.

42

Kim Jong-un says he wants to advance technology, to move North Korean students and jobs into the future. In 2009, only about one of every 100 North Koreans used a cell phone. Most stand in line to use public phones in the city. In the countryside they simply do without. In 2008, Kim Jung-il partnered with Egyptian communications company Orascom to build Koryolink, a mobile phone network. Even in this impoverished country, smartphones creep in, beginning with one seen on Kim Jong-un's desk in 2013. Internet use has increased, as wealthier North Koreans in Pyongyang use their cell phones to schedule meetings, read e-books about Kim Il-sung, and share pictures of their kids or their favorite MP3s.[1] But phone calls are only allowed within North Korea. Even at North Korean universities, the government completely blocks access to the international internet. People can only access North Korean sites. As technology seeps into the country, will Kim Jong-un be able to keep North Korea's walls of isolation high?

FYI FACT:

Fun and useful Korean phrases:

Hello – *Annyeong*
Nice to meet you – *Mannaseo bangawoyo*
Goodbye – *Anneyong kyeseyo*
Yes – *Ne*
No - *Aniyo*
Awesome! – *A-sa!*
Delicious! – *Massissoyo!*
Where is the restroom? – *Hwajangshil i odi issoyu?*
Thank you – *Gomapsumnida.*
I am going to Pyongyang – *Nanun Pyongyang-e gamnida.*
Long live the *Juche* idea! – *Juche sasang-manse!*
Americans are wolves in human form – *Yankingum in gane tarul sun sunnyang-ida*

Source: Robert Willoughby, *North Korea: The Bradt Travel Guide* (Bucks, United Kingdom: Bradt Travel Guides Ltd., 2008), pp. 219-221.

Students of the prestigious art school, the Kim Won-gyun Conservatory in Pyongyang, perform the opera *Eugene Onegin* by Russian composer Peter Tchaikovsky.

Chapter 9

Everyday Life in North Korea

On paper, North Koreans appear to have a good life. Everyone has free access to state doctors—if they can walk to the clinic and if hospitals have working electricity and plumbing. But while the average South Korean lives to be 81, older than the average in the U.S. or Canada, the average North Korean only lives to be 69. Hunger, stress, or cruel prison sentences shorten many lives.

An unusually harsh winter in 2010–2011 destroyed cold-weather crops like barley, wheat, and potatoes.[1] Farmers planted corn that spring, only to lose those crops to record-breaking summer rains. The famine of 2011 left even soldiers bullying poor villagers for food. Because most North Koreans rely on a diet of boiled corn and potatoes, the United Nations estimated that out of North Korea's 28 million people, nearly 16 million went hungry in 2013. A meal with meat is rare. In mountain cities, people raise dogs, and not as pets. The Korean favorite dish, *kimchi*—spicy pickled cabbage and vegetables—does not provide many calories, but it remains a popular way to make bland food tasty, especially since it stays fresh for the 90% of North Koreans who do not own a refrigerator.

In times of famine, children are the hardest hit. One out of every four children in North Korea are so starved that their growth is stunted. The average 14-year-old North Korean boy, for example, raised on thin broth made from corn and weeds, is five inches (13 centimeters) shorter than a South Korean boy fed on cheeseburgers and milkshakes. Untold numbers of North Korean orphans have no choice but to live on the

The Ryugyong Hotel (at the far right) dominates the Pyongyang skyline. Construction on the 105-story structure began in 1987, was halted five years later, and resumed in 2008. It is not clear when it will open.

streets and beg for scraps at markets that are already empty.[2] Their parents may have died of starvation, or been sent away to prison camp.

There is no way of knowing how many prison camps exist, or how many prisoners rot within them. Some reports use satellite images to estimate that as many as 130,000 North Koreans were held prisoner in 2013.[3] Of those who are not executed, up to 40% will die from overwork, starvation, beatings, or torture.

A fortunate few North Koreans have escaped. Born in 1969, Kang Chol-hwan was sent to the Yodok prison camp when he was 9. His grandfather was accused of spying for the Japanese, so the entire family was imprisoned. They ate rats or worms. Prison guards viciously beat children like Chol-hwan, and forced him to watch as they killed those in the camp who did not behave. After 10 hard years, Chol-whan and his family were sent home. But he dreamed of escape. He and a friend from Yodok snuck across the Yalu River into China in 1992. He moved to South Korea and wrote a book about his experience, *The Aquariums*

of Pyongyang, giving the world a first look at life inside a North Korean prison camp.

Compared to the mysterious, dangerous, hungry countryside, the capital city of Pyongyang seems like a different world—one with food and daytime electricity. Nowhere else on earth can you find a city of over 2 million people so completely free of trash and graffiti. Homeless, orphans, and beggars have been swept out of view. North Koreans must get permission to live in the capital city, so those who don't fit with the government's perfect image are assigned a different hometown.

In the daytime, workers maintain the city's schools, government offices, museums and monuments, parks, and restaurants. If they have time, and money from their small government allowance, Pyongyang residents might visit one of the few shops. Ladies will go without rice to splurge on makeup and haircuts. For larger purchases, like Chinese-made laptops or sneakers, North Koreans need to get special permission from the *imminban* first. On Sundays, families might rollerblade at a park, visit the zoo, see a movie made by Kim Jong-il, or take in one of Kim Il-sung's original operas. One of the most famous operas is *The Sea of Blood*, which tells of a farm wife whose husband and children are slaughtered by Japanese soldiers. Instead of giving herself over to grief, she channels her anger into revolution. The Pyongyang Grand Theater has staged *The Sea of Blood* three or four times every week since July 1971.

North Koreans love music, and many play instruments. Traditional Korean instruments like the *geomungo*, a zither, or the *sohaegeum*, a four-stringed fiddle, have been replaced as the Kims sought to create modern Western-style classical orchestras. Kim Jong-un's wife, Ri Sol-ju, was once a singer with the Unhasu Orchestra. North Korean radio

The *geomungo*, a traditional 11-stringed Korean zither

plays Unhansu Orchestra songs like "Family of the General," as well as pop songs like "Whistle" and "We Shall Hold Our Bayonets More Firmly" by government-formed girl-bands like the Wangjaesan Light Music Band and the Pochonbo Electric Ensemble. These groups broke up after lead singer Hyon Song-wol was executed in 2013.

Pyongyang celebrates official holidays, as well as important Korean folk ones. During the spring holiday of Tano, families dress in colorful clothes, perhaps even wearing a traditional Korean belted robe, the *hanbok*, and play outdoor games like tug-of-war. Koreans honor their ancestors during the fall harvest. After visiting the graves of loved ones, families share memories over a meal of rice with fresh vegetables and fruit. The most important Korean holiday is Seollal, a three-day celebration of the lunar new year in January or February. Koreans play games like *yut nori* and enjoy a traditional dinner of rice cakes, dumpling soup, and fruit punch. Children gather for family stories at the feet of their elders, who reward their listeners with treats.

Night is dark and quiet, even in Pyongyang. To save power, all the lights go out except for spotlights that shine on stadiums, museums, and public art like Kim Il-sung's statue. One exception is the Kaeson Fun Fair, a massive amusement park that beckons fun-seekers all day and night with carousels, roller coasters, and other rides. North Korea boasts older amusement parks, but many rides, like North Korea itself, have gone rusty from years of neglect.

The Kaeson Fun Fair, an amusement park in Pyongyang

A 65-foot (20-meter) bronze statue of Kim Il-sung towers in front of a mural of Mount Paektu at the Mansudae Grand Monument in Pyongyang.

Can We Visit
North Korea?

In 2013, North Korea's International Tourism Company announced plans to open the country to tourists, even Americans. That year, U.S. basketball star Dennis Rodman paid two visits to Kim Jong-un, his new friend and basketball fan.

However, the U.S. State Department warns Westerners to stay out of North Korea. Inside the country or at the border, any one, at any time, can be jailed or deported for speaking out against the government. In 2012, U.S. citizen Kenneth Bae was sentenced to 15 years in a prison camp for carrying a laptop with pictures of starving North Korean children.

If you go, your trip will be carefully controlled. The North Korean government wants to showcase the best of what the country has to offer. No tourists can enter without a DPRK-approved tour group. Each group gets a handpicked tour guide who is fluent in both foreign languages and *juche* philosophy. Talking to ordinary North Korean citizens, or trying to visit a place without permission, could land you in jail as a suspected spy.

Shorter trips will stay in Pyongyang. The first stop of any tour will be the Mansudae Grand Monument, an enormous bronze statue of Kim Il-sung. The Great Leader commissioned the 65-foot (20-meter) statue in celebration of his 60th birthday in 1972. Plaques near the statue read "Long live Kim Il-sung!" and "Let Us Drive out U.S. Imperialism and Reunify the Country."[1] Your tour guides will tell you,

Kim Il-sung and Kim Jong-il lie in their final resting places at the Kumsusan Memorial Palace in Pyongyang.

in worshipful tones, of the many wonderful deeds of Kim and his family. You must bow and lay flowers at the statue's feet.

Visit the Victorious Fatherland Liberation War Museum to see the Korean War through North Korea's eyes, a side nearly always neglected by Western history books. Many rooms of stunning exhibits include not just photos and documents, but also actual U.S. tanks, British torpedo boats, and North Korean warplanes.[2]

In the elaborate Kumsusan Palace of the Sun, the Kims' bodies are preserved and put on display under glass coffins. The dead leaders now have new titles—Kim Il-sun is called "Eternal Leader," while Kim Jong-il is "Eternal General Secretary of the Workers' Party" and "Eternal Chairman of the National Defense Commission."

In late July or August, you must see the Arirang Mass Games. The largest stadium in the world, the 150,000-seat May Day stadium, holds both spectators and performers. This theatrical, athletic, and musical

**Juche Tower
in Pyongyang**

production earned a spot as the world's largest in the 2007 *Guinness Book of World Records.* Tens of thousands of highly trained performers, most of them school children who have rehearsed for months, put on a tightly choreographed spectacle of music, dance, gymnastics, art, beauty, and devotion to the Kim family. Special performers hold up colored cards at precise times and places, like pixels on a computer screen, to form detailed pictures. The final act is dedicated to international friendship.

Your last stop is a beacon along the Taedong River. The Great Leader designed the Juche Tower, using one block for every day of his 70-year life. Statues in front show three Koreans standing united: a worker with a hammer, a farmer with a sickle, and a scholar holding a brush for calligraphy. Take the elevator 560 feet (170 meters) to the tower's top, just below a torch which is kept constantly lit, for a breathtaking view of the capital.

For a longer tour, you might head 90 miles (150 kilometers) north into the stunning green mountains of Myohyangsan, home of the International

A section of one of the murals formed during the Arirang Mass Games in August 2012. Thousands of people in the stands held up cards to form this image.

The Songdowon Children's Camp, held near Wonson each summer since 1960, hosts 1,200 international children in a cultural exchange camp. The best North Korean students interact with children from countries like Russia, China, Mongolia, Thailand, Syria, Nigeria, Tanzania, and Mexico.

Friendship Exhibition. This unusual museum holds collections of gifts given to Kim Il-sung and Kim Jong-il, and includes everything from gem-encrusted swords to gun-shaped liquor bottles. Or you may drive 125 miles (200 kilometers) east, to the lovely coastal beaches like Wonsan or Lake Sijung. Ask to travel 80 miles (130 kilometers) further, south of Wonsan, to Mt. Kumgang, or Diamond Mountain. This national park and historic temple site is a favorite vacation resort of the Kims.

Visit the Joint Security Area in the village of Panmunjeom for a solemn end to your tour. Staggered across the 38th parallel, like a scar across the peninsula, 1,292 identical rusty signs mark the Korean Demilitarized Zone (DMZ). Guard towers and untold numbers of unexploded landmines mark the southern border of North Korea, about 100 miles (160 kilometers) south of Pyongyang. The South Korean capital of Seoul lies less than 35 miles (56 kilometers) away. Panmunjeom is the site of the North Korea Peace Museum, a building constructed in just five days to house the signing of the Korean Armistice Agreement. The actual border between the two Koreas opens at this spot. Crisply uniformed armed guards from the two countries stare each other down 24 hours a day. They are close enough to walk over and shake hands, yet so far apart in the way they live today.

A trip to North Korea is an eye-opening adventure. The friendly guides seem more open than you would expect for people who are supposed to speak only from a rehearsed script about the greatness of their leader. But the perfection of what the government chooses for you to see makes you wonder—what about the North Korea you didn't see?

Mul Naengmyun

(Korean Cold Noodles)

Once a delicacy served to Choson kings in Pyongyang, *naengmyun* (or "cold noodles") spread in popularity throughout the peninsula after the Korean War. This freezing cold, sweet-and-sour soup uses that can be stored through the winter season—from the buckwheat and potato in the chewy *naengmyun* noodles, to the pear and pickled radish. Today, Koreans enjoy this refreshing soup throughout the year. You can find *naengmyun* noodles and other ingredients, such as brown rice vinegar, pickled radish, and Korean hot mustard (if you dare!) in specialty or Asian grocery stores.

Ingredients:

¼ pound *naengyun* noodles (or substitute Japanese soba noodles)
4 cups broth (made with noodle spice packet, or use beef or vegetable broth)
1-inch piece of fresh ginger, peeled and sliced
1 clove garlic, sliced
1 green onion, cut into 1-inch pieces
2-3 tablespoons brown rice vinegar (or substitute white vinegar)
1 egg, hardboiled and sliced
½ cucumber, seeded and julienned
1 small Asian pear, peeled and sliced thinly
¼ cup pickled radish (optional)
sesame seeds (optional)
Korean mustard or other hot mustard (optional)

Instructions:

Prepare the following recipe with adult supervision:

1. Cook noodles according to package directions. Drain and rinse immediately in cold water. Mound noodles into serving bowls and refrigerate.
2. Combine broth, ginger, garlic, onion, and vinegar in a saucepan. Bring to a boil, then reduce heat and simmer, uncovered, for 30 minutes. Remove ginger and garlic. Cool broth; refrigerate until cold, at least one hour.
3. Remove noodles from refrigerator. Ladle the cold broth over the noodles. Top with the garnishes: cucumber, sliced pear, pickled radish (optional), sesame seeds (optional), and, for an authentic (and spicy!) experience, Korean hot mustard.

This traditional two-player board game is especially popular during Korean New Year celebrations. To play *yut*, you need a game board (*mal-pan*), four game pieces (*mal*) per player, and *yut*-sticks. Make your own *yut-nori* game set and enjoy hours of fun with your family and friends!

Materials

- Plain cloth square, at least 8" on one side
- Cardboard, larger than the cloth square
- Pencil
- Ruler
- Sharpie pens or fabric markers
- 4 popsicle sticks
- 2 sets of game pieces—each set must contain 4 identical, small, flat-sided objects (like buttons or coins)

Instructions

1. Lay the cloth on top of the cardboard. Using the pencil, copy the following board design onto the cloth. Make each side of the game board 8 inches (about 20 centimeters) long. Use a ruler as a guide to help you make straight lines.
2. Trace over your pencil marks with Sharpie markers. Use any colors to finish your game board.
3. Using the markers, write "UP" on one face of each popsicle stick, and, if you like, decorate that face the same way on each stick. Now, flip all the sticks over, and decorate the other faces using a different design. The finished popsicle sticks will each have a front and a back that are different from each other, like heads and tails on a coin.

Now you are ready to play! The rules are simple, like the board game "Sorry!" Grab one, two, or three friends, and your game pieces, or mal. Pick a corner of the board to be your "home." Each of your pieces starts there, and moves around the board in the same direction. The goal is to be the first player to move all four mal away from his or her corner "home" and then back again.

When it's your turn, throw your *yut* sticks and move one of your *mal*:
- 1 space (*do*)
- 2 spaces (*gae*)
- 3 spaces (*geol*)
- 4 spaces (*yut*)
- 5 spaces (*mo*)

You must start moving around the outside of the board, but if you land on another corner, you can take a shortcut across one of the diagonals. If you land exactly on another player's *mal*, they take their piece off the board and have to start that *mal* from home again. If you land exactly on your own *mal*, those two pieces can join forces and move together like one—getting home twice as fast! But if another player lands on your double *mal*, both pieces have to start over again. Have fun playing again and again!

Source: Steve Miller, "How to Play Yut Nori (Korean Game)" http://www.youtube.com/watch?v=G90o0ai57EM

Yut-Nori Board Game

Dates BCE

2333	Mythical reign of Dangun begins.
108	Han Dynasty of China conquers Korean Peninsula.
57 BCE–	
668 CE	Three Kingdoms period: Koguryo Dynasty rules the north, while Silla and Paekche rule the south.

Dates CE

668–936	Silla conquers most of the Korean Peninsula.
918–1392	Koryo Dynasty unites Korea.
1392–1910	Choson Dynasty controls Korea.
1904–1905	Russia and Japan go to war over control of Korea.
1910–1945	Japan occupies the Korean Peninsula.
1945	After Japan is defeated in World War II, Korea is split along the 38th parallel.
1948	North Korea becomes the Democratic People's Republic of Korea, governed by Kim Il-sung.
1950–1953	North Korea and South Korea, backed by their allies, fight against each other in the Korean War.
1985	North Korea agrees to the Nuclear Nonproliferation-Treaty, pledging never to develop nuclear weapons and to allow open international inspections.
1993	North Korea withdraws from the Nuclear Nonproliferation Treaty.
1994	Kim Il-sung dies and his son Kim Jong-il becomes North Korea's leader.
2002	U.S. President George W. Bush calls North Korea part of an "axis of evil," along with Iran and Iraq; North Korea admits to building nuclear weapons using uranium from its power plants.
2003	Six-Nation talks begin among North Korea, the U.S., China, Russia, Japan, and South Korea in an effort to get North Korea to disarm its nuclear program in exchange for aid for its people.
2006	North Korea detonates its first nuclear weapon.
2008	Six-Nation talks fail to reach an agreement on inspection of North Korea's nuclear facilities.
2009	North Korea launches a long-range rocket over the Pacific Ocean.
2010	North Korea sinks the *Cheonan*, a South Korean naval vessel.
2011	Kim Jong-il dies of a heart attack; his third son, Kim Jong-un, becomes leader after two weeks of national mourning.
2012	Kim Jong-un agrees to allow international observers access to North Korea's nuclear facilities.
2013	North Korea conducts a third nuclear test; Kim Jong-un invites U.S. basketball star Dennis Rodman to visit.
2014	North and South Korea have agreed to hold reunions of families separated since the Korean War.

Chapter 1. A Country Split in Two
1. Robert Johnson, "Check Out These Twisted North Korean Propaganda Posters," *Business Insider*, December 20, 2011.
2. Justin Berkowitz, "Cars from the 'Axis of Evil': North Korea," *Car and Driver*, August 2010.
3. Malcolm Moore, "As Pyongyang Celebrates, British Aid Worker Reveals Poverty of Rural North Korea," *The Telegraph*, July 27, 2013.
4. Patrick Boehler, "Unicorns' Existence Proven, Says North Korea," *Time*, November 30, 2012.

Chapter 2. Land of the Morning Calm
1. Tom O'Neill, "North Korea: Facts on the Ground," *National Geographic News*, April 6, 2013.
2. Global Volcanism Program. "Changbaishan." http://www.volcano.si.edu/world/volcano.cfm?vnum=1005-06-
3. Julian Ryall, "Kim Jong-un Wants to Build a 'World Class' Ski Resort in North Korea," *The Telegraph*, May 27, 2013.

Chapter 3. The Rise of Choson
1. Kidong Bae, "Peopling the Korean Peninsula," in *Asian Paleoanthropology: from Africa to China and Beyond*, Eds. Christopher J. Norton and David R. Braun (New York: Springer, 2010), p. 181.
2. *The History of Nations: North Korea*, Ed. Debra A. Miller (Farmington Hills, Michigan: Greenhaven Press, 2004), p. 15.

Chapter 4. The Foreign Fate of the Hermit Kingdom
1. Martin J. Gannon and Rajnandini Pillai, *Understanding Global Cultures* (Los Angeles: Sage Publications, Inc., 2013), p. 126.
2. Bethany Lacina and Nils Petter Gleditsch, "Monitoring Trends in Global Combat: A New Dataset of Battle Deaths," *European Journal of Population*, Volume 21, Issue 2–3, June 2005, p. 154.
3. R.J. Rummel, Statistics of *Democide: Genocide and Mass Murder since 1900* (Munich, Germany: LIT Verlag, 1998), p. 179.
4. Ibid., p. 179.

Chapter 5. The Democratic People's Republic of Korea and Juche
1. Democratic People's Republic of Korea Official Webpage, http://www.korea-dpr.com/
2. Choe Sang-hun, "Sexist Taunt From North Korea Raises Gender Issue for the South's New Leader," *New York Times*, March 14, 2013.
3. Chris Evans, "North Korean Cinema: Kim Jong-il's Movie Mania," *The Independent*, June 14, 2013.

Chapter 6. The Culture and Religion of the Kims
1. B. R. Myers, "North Korea's Race Problem: What I Learned from Reading Kim Jong Il's Propaganda," *Foreign Policy*, March/April 2010, http://www.foreignpolicy.com/articles/2010/02/22/north_koreas_race_problem
2. Ibid.
3. Margo DeMello, *Faces Around the World: A Cultural Encyclopedia of the Human Face* (Santa Barbara, Calif.: ABC-CLIO, 2012), p.198.
4. Barbara Demick, *Nothing to Envy: Ordinary Lives in North Korea* (New York: Spiegel & Grau, 2009), p. 53.
5. Tom O'Neill, "North Korea: Facts on the Ground," *National Geographic News*, April 6, 2013.

Chapter 7. Nuclear-Powered Economy

1. United States Central Intelligence Agency, "Korea, North," *The CIA World Factbook*, https://www.cia.gov/library/publications/the-world-factbook/geos/kn.html
2. Barbara Demick, *Nothing to Envy: Ordinary Lives in North Korea* (New York: Spiegel & Grau, 2009), p. 59.
3. "North Korea: A Country Study," United States Library of Congress, http://lcweb2.loc.gov/frd/cs/pdf/CS_North-Korea.pdf
4. World Bank, "Korea, Dem. Rep," http://data.worldbank.org/country/korea-democratic-republic
5. Ibid.
6. Stephen Mihm, "No Ordinary Counterfeit," *New York Times*, July 23, 2006.

Chapter 8. Training Young Pioneers

1. Jean Lee, "'Hello world': First tweet sent from a cellphone in North Korea as Pyongyang offers mobile Internet service to foreigners," *National Post*, February 27, 2013, http://bit.ly/15RBfcf

Chapter 9. Everyday Life in North Korea

1. Malcolm Moore, "As Pyongyang Celebrates, British Aid Worker Reveals Poverty of Rural North Korea," *The Telegraph*, July 27, 2013.
2. Madison Park, "Orphaned and Homeless: Surviving the Streets of North Korea," CNN, May 14, 2013, http://www.cnn.com/2013/05/13/world/asia/north-korea-orphans/index.html
3. Julian Ryall, "Up to 20,000 North Korean Prison Camp Inmates Have 'Disappeared' Says Human Rights Group." *The Telegraph*, September 5, 2013. http://www.telegraph.co.uk/news/worldnews/asia/northkorea/10288945/Up-to-20000-North-Korean-prison-camp-inmates-have-disappeared-says-human-rights-group.html

Chapter 10. Can We Visit North Korea?

1. Robert Willoughby, *North Korea: The Bradt Travel Guide* (Bucks, UK: Bradt Travel Guides Ltd., 2008), p. 114.
2. Ibid., p. 118.

FURTHER READING

Books

Hart, Joyce. *Kim Jong Il: Leader of North Korea*. New York: Rosen Publishing, 2008.
Kummer, Patricia K. *North Korea*. New York: Children's Press, 2008.
Raum, Elizabeth. *North Korea*. Chicago: Heinemann Library, 2012.
Rice, Earle. *Overview of the Korean War*. Hockessin, Del.: Mitchell Lane, 2009.
Salter, Christopher L. *North Korea*. New York: Chelsea House, 2007.
Worth, Richard. *Kim Jong Il*. New York: Chelsea House, 2008.

On the Internet

Democratic People's Republic of Korea Official Webpage
    http://www.korea-dpr.com/
DPRK Profile – Koryo Tourism
    http://www.koryogroup.com/dprk_profile.php
First Steps
    http://www2.firststepscanada.org/
Korean Friendship Association USA
    http://www.kfausa.org
Liberty in North Korea
    http://libertyinnorthkorea.org/
MercyCorps: North Korea
    http://www.mercycorps.org/north-korea

Bae, Kidong. "Peopling the Korean Peninsula." *Asian Paleoanthropology: from Africa to China and Beyond.* Eds. Christopher J. Norton and David R. Braun. New York: Springer, 2010.

Berkowitz, Justin. "Cars from the 'Axis of Evil': North Korea." *Car and Driver*, August 2010. http://www.caranddriver.com/features/cars-from-north-korea-features

Boehler, Patrick. "Unicorns' Existence Proven, Says North Korea." *Time*, November 30, 2012. http://newsfeed.time.com/2012/11/30/unicorns-existence-proven-says-north-korea/

Choe Sang-hun. "Sexist Taunt From North Korea Raises Gender Issue for the South's New Leader." *New York Times*, March 14, 2013. http://www.nytimes.com/2013/03/15/world/asia/north-koreas-sexist-barb-stirs-gender-issue-in-south.html?ref=world

DeMello, Margo. *Faces Around the World: A Cultural Encyclopedia of the Human Face.* Santa Barbara, Calif.: ABC-CLIO, 2012.

Demick, Barbara. *Nothing to Envy: Ordinary Lives in North Korea.* New York: Spiegel & Grau, 2009.

Evans, Chris. "North Korean Cinema: Kim Jong-il's Movie Mania." *The Independent*, June 14, 2013. http://www.independent.co.uk/arts-entertainment/films/features/north-korean-cinema-kim-jongils-movie-mania-8657673.html

Gannon, Martin J. and Rajnandini Pillai. *Understanding Global Cultures.* 5th Edition. Los Angeles: Sage Publications, 2013.

Global Volcanism Program. "Changbaishan." http://www.volcano.si.edu/world/volcano.cfm?vnum=1005-06-

The History of Nations: North Korea. Ed. Debra A. Miller. Farmington Hills, Michigan: Greenhaven Press, 2004.

Lacina, Bethany and Nils Petter Gleditsch. "Monitoring Trends in Global Combat: A New Dataset of Battle Deaths." *European Journal of Population*, Volume 21, Issue 2–3, June 2005, pp. 145–166.

Lee, Jean. "'Hello world': First tweet sent from a cellphone in North Korea as Pyongyang offers mobile Internet service to foreigners." *National Post*, February 27, 2013. http://bit.ly/15RBfcf

Moore, Malcolm. "As Pyongyang Celebrates, British Aid Worker Reveals Poverty of Rural North Korea." *The Telegraph*, July 27, 2013. http://www.telegraph.co.uk/news/worldnews/asia/northkorea/10206210/As-Pyongyang-celebrates-British-aid-worker-reveals-poverty-of-rural-North-Korea.html

Myers, B. R. "North Korea's Race Problem: What I Learned from Reading Kim Jong Il's Propaganda." *Foreign Policy*, March/April 2010. http://www.foreignpolicy.com/articles/2010/02/22/north_koreas_race_problem

Mihm, Stephen. "No Ordinary Counterfeit." *New York Times*, July 23, 2006. http://www.nytimes.com/2006/07/23/magazine/23counterfeit.html?pagewanted=all&_r=0

"North Korea – Educational System – overview." http://education.stateuniversity.com/pages/1113/North-Korea-EDUCATIONAL-SYSTEM-OVERVIEW.html

O'Neill, Tom. "North Korea: Facts on the Ground." *National Geographic News*, April 6, 2013.

Park, Madison. "Orphaned and Homeless: Surviving the Streets of North Korea." CNN, May 14, 2013. http://www.cnn.com/2013/05/13/world/asia/north-korea-orphans/index.html.

Rummel, R.J. *Statistics of Democide: Genocide and Mass Murder since 1900.* Munich, Germany: LIT Verlag, 1998.

Ryall, Julian. "Up to 20,000 North Korean Prison Camp Inmates Have 'Disappeared' Says Human Rights Group." *The Telegraph*, September 5, 2013. http://www.telegraph.co.uk/news/worldnews/asia/northkorea/10288945/Up-to-20000-North-Korean-prison-camp-inmates-have-disappeared-says-human-rights-group.html

United Nations Statistics Division. "UNdata." July 5, 2013, http://data.un.org/Data.aspx?d=POP&f=tableCode%3A240

United States Central Intelligence Agency. "Korea, North." in *The CIA World Factbook.* https://www.cia.gov/library/publications/the-world-factbook/geos/kn.html

United States Library of Congress. "North Korea: A Country Study." http://lcweb2.loc.gov/frd/cs/pdf/CS_North-Korea.pdf

Willoughby, Robert. *North Korea: The Bradt Travel Guide.* Bucks, United Kingdom: Bradt Travel Guides, 2008.

World Bank. "Korea, Dem. Rep." http://data.worldbank.org/country/korea-democratic-republic

armistice (AHR-miss-tuss)—Truce between opposing sides in a war.

brinksmanship (BRINKS-man-ship)—Pushing a dangerous situation to the limit of safety in order to gain an advantage.

calligraphy (kuh-LIHG-ruh-fee)—The art of fine writing, often using a brush.

celadon (SELL-uh-don)—Pale gray-green.

communism (CAHM-myoo-nizm)—A social system in which the economy is completely controlled by the government.

dictator (DIK-tay-tor)—A ruler who controls every aspect of government.

dolmen (DOHL-men)—A tomb made from several large rock slabs to form a table-like structure.

dynasty (DIE-nuh-stee)—A series of rulers from the same family.

gulag (GOO-lahg)—A prison camp that forces inmates to do hard work in miserable conditions.

kibun (kee-BOON—Reputation of one's family or self.

monsoon (mon-SOON)—Predictable seasonal winds that bring changes in weather.

propaganda (prop-uh-GAN-duh)—Posters, newspaper articles, radio broadcasts, or TV shows that spread information or ideas to help a government and harm another government.

reneged (ree-NEGGED)—Broke a promise.

sanctions (SANK-shuns)—Punishments.

totalitarian (toe-tall-ih-TARE-ee-un)—A system of government that demands complete obedience from its citizens and allows no personal freedoms.

Claire O'Neal has written over two dozen books for Mitchell Lane, including *We Visit Yemen*, *We Visit Iraq*, and *We Visit Libya*. She holds degrees in English and biology from Indiana University and a Ph.D. in chemistry from the University of Washington. Claire loves to travel, and has visited Great Britain and New Zealand. She lives in Delaware with her husband and two young boys while dreaming up her next globetrotting adventure.